Brooks Library Media Center
2700 Stonebridge Blvd.
Aurora, IL 60504

90581

W9-AAE-596

Our Endangered Planet
OCEANS

Mary Hoff
and
Mary M. Rodgers

Brooks Library Media Center
2700 Stonebridge Blvd.
Aurora, IL 60504

LERNER PUBLICATIONS COMPANY • MINNEAPOLIS

Thanks to Dr. Joseph Shapiro, Dr. Chris Paola, James E. Laib, Kerstin Coyle, Zachary Marell, and Gary Hansen for their help in preparing this book.

Words that appear in **bold** type are listed in a glossary that starts on page 67.

Copyright © 1991 Lerner Publications Company

All rights reserved. International copyright secured. No part of this book may be reproduced, stored in a retrieval system, or transmitted in any form or by any means—electronic, mechanical, photocopying, recording, or otherwise—without the prior written permission of the publisher, except for the inclusion of brief quotations in an acknowledged review.

This book is available in two editions:
Library binding by Lerner Publications Company
Soft cover by First Avenue Editions
241 First Avenue North
Minneapolis, MN 55401

ISBN: 0–8225–2505–4 (lib. bdg.)
ISBN: 0–8225–9628–8 (pbk.)

LIBRARY OF CONGRESS CATALOGING-IN-PUBLICATION DATA

Hoff, Mary King.
      Our endangered planet. Oceans / Mary Hoff and Mary M. Rodgers.
         p.   cm.
      Includes bibliographical references and index.
      Summary: Describes concisely the global uses and abuses of the world's oceans and seas.
      ISBN 0-8225-2505-4 (lib. bdg.)
      1. Ocean—Juvenile literature. [1. Ocean.] I. Rodgers, Mary M. (Mary Madeline), 1954–   II. Title. III. Title: Oceans.
GC21.5.H64 1991
333.91'64—dc20   91–11384
                                                                CIP
                                                                AC

Manufactured in the United States of America

2 3 4 5 6 7 8 9 10 00 99 98 97 96 95 94 93

Front cover: Foamy spray and powerful waves are familiar traits of the Pacific Ocean, the largest of the world's five oceans. Back cover: (Left) Strong, high waves propel a South African surfer toward the shore of the Indian Ocean. (Right) The ocean's movements can also bring oil spills onto beaches making a coastal mess, such as this one in Texas.

Recycled paper

All paper used in this book is of recycled material and may be recycled.

Recyclable

CONTENTS

OUR ENDANGERED PLANET

In the 1960s, astronauts first traveled beyond earth's protective atmosphere and were able to look back at our planet. What they saw was a beautiful globe, turning slowly in space. That image reminds us that our home planet has limits, for we know of no other place that can support life.

The various parts of our natural environment—including air, water, soil, plants, and animals—are partners in making our planet a good place to live. If we endanger one element, the other partners are badly affected, too.

People throughout the world are working to protect and heal earth's environment. They recognize that making nature our ally and not our victim is the way to shape a common future. Because we have only one planet to share, its health and survival mean that we all can live.

One of the earth's main surface elements is water. In fact, water covers about three-fourths of our planet. Nearly all of this water is salty and lies in oceans and seas. Humans have long used oceans to provide food and transportation.

We have also found other ways to use—and misuse—oceans. For example, they have become a global dumping ground for our garbage. We have begun to catch fish in such great amounts that there are fewer fish left to have babies. As a result, supplies of some kinds of fish are decreasing. Ships that transport oil have released their greasy cargo into the ocean, hurting many types of wildlife that depend on oceans for survival. People are studying these problems to find solutions. The more we understand the ocean, the more active we can be in helping to preserve it for future generations.

CHAPTER ONE

THE BIG PICTURE

When we want to talk about something BIG, we often mention oceans. They cover the biggest part of our planet—nearly 145 million square miles (375 million square kilometers). This area is more than 40 times the size of the United States. Oceans also hold 97 percent of all the water in the entire world!

In addition to being vast, oceans are extremely deep, averaging about two and a half miles (four kilometers) in depth. How does that compare with the distance between your home and school?

(Left) **The huge Pacific Ocean dwarfs a couple walking along the coast of Oregon.** *(Right)* **A deep-sea squid produces light in the darkness of the ocean's depths using tiny organs in its body.**

COASTAL CLUES

When we imagine an ocean, most of us think of the part that we can see—a huge expanse of choppy water stretching from the shore to the **horizon.** If you live in Keflavík, Iceland, you know what the edge of an ocean might look like. It may be rocky and rough. In Florida, on the other hand, the shore may be smooth and sandy. If you enjoy suntanning, you prob-

A gently rounded bay forms part of the coast of Madagascar, an island in the Indian Ocean off the eastern coast of Africa.

The constant force of the rough North Sea, an arm of the North Atlantic Ocean, has shaped the rocky cliffs of Duncansby Head in northern Scotland.

ably like beaches, such as those in Hawaii, Spain, and Brazil.

Geographers—people who study the earth's physical features—give different names to the various shapes an ocean's

Liberia, a nation in West Africa, has a long coast along the South Atlantic Ocean. At some places, lagoons lie near the shore across a narrow barrier of land.

shoreline can take. Perhaps you have seen a bay—a sheltered dent in the coastline. A gulf is a larger curve that is partly surrounded by land.

Bays and gulfs can be home to **estuaries**—places where fresh-water rivers flow from inland areas into the ocean. The fresh water, which contains very little salt, mixes with the ocean's salty water to create a special, food-rich **habitat** (natural home) for many animals and plants.

If you live in Norway or New Zealand, you might be in a rugged area shaped by **glaciers.** These slow-moving masses of ice have carved long, narrow estuaries called **fjords. Lagoons** are another kind of estuary, where an offshore barrier, such as a sandbar or an island, protects the shore from the wind and waves of the open sea. Our planet also has smaller salt-water passages, including **straits, channels,** and **sounds.**

We can see all of these parts of the ocean through exploration or on maps. But "the big picture" is really much bigger. The ocean we see at the surface is just the thin layer of an incredible world that exists beneath the waves.

Like dry land, oceans have mountains, plains, and valleys. The ocean floor even contains active underwater volcanoes that spew up red-hot lava. As more and more of the hot lava erupts and cools, it builds up on the ocean floor until it breaks the surface of the water. Surtsey Island, a volcanic landform off the southern coast of Iceland, first appeared above the North Atlantic Ocean's surface in 1963.

Surtsey Island, a volcanic island in the North Atlantic Ocean, resulted from underwater eruptions that still produce red-hot lava and steam.

Among the ocean's fascinating creatures are hardy Sally Lightfoot crabs (left) that survive the movement of rough waves and delicate plants (right) that live in the depths of the Middle East's Red Sea.

SALTY DIFFERENCES

Unlike lakes and rivers, which hold fresh water, oceans contain salty water. Natural chemicals—mostly sodium and chloride—make ocean water salty. There are also small amounts of about 70 other chemicals.

Most maps of the world show five oceans. The largest ocean—the Pacific—separates North and South America from Asia and Australia. The Atlantic Ocean stretches between Europe, Africa, and the Americas. The Indian Ocean extends along the south side of Asia from Africa to Australia. The icy Arctic Ocean surrounds the North Pole. At the bottom of our planet is the Southern Ocean, which encircles the continent of Antarctica, where the South Pole lies.

Even though sailors and scientists have given names to five oceans, these bodies of water are not really separate. The imaginary line we draw to split the Atlantic from the Pacific, for example, is a map-maker's invention.

Some oceanographers—people who study oceans—think we should recognize only three oceans, making the Arctic and Southern oceans parts of the other oceans. Most geographers, however, talk about five separate oceans. People sometimes discuss oceans and seas as if they were the same thing. But, to scientists, these names describe different salt-water areas.

Seas are smaller than oceans. Between Europe and North Africa is the Mediterranean Sea. The Sargasso Sea lies in the North Atlantic Ocean. The North Sea stretches between Great Britain and northwestern Europe. On either side of the Red Sea sit Egypt and Saudi Arabia. Scientists have noted more than 50 additional seas around the world.

The important point to remember is that whatever happens to one ocean affects all oceans. This is why we refer to "the ocean"—the world ocean—rather than to a specific ocean when we talk about all of the world's salt water.

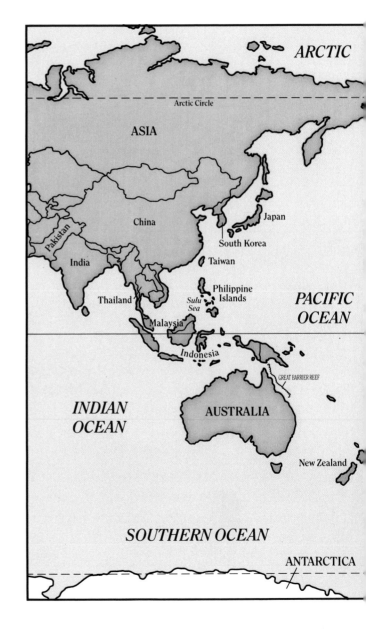

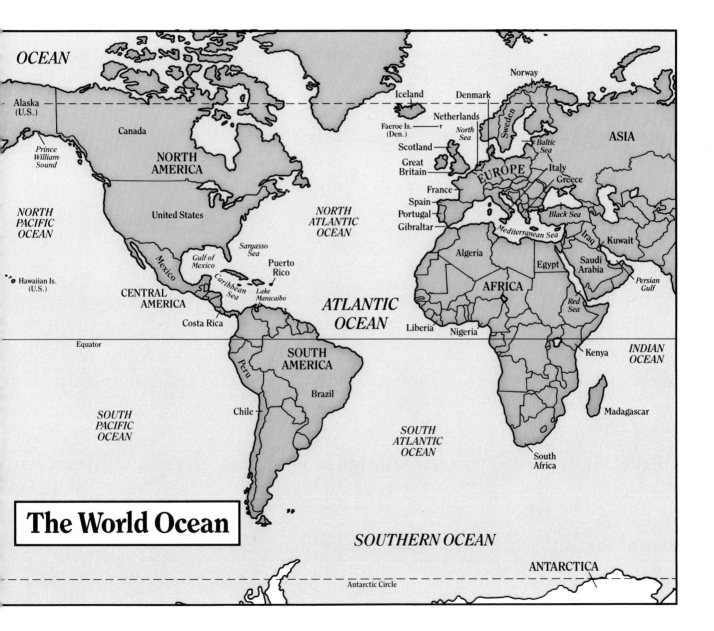

The World Ocean

OCEAN

Alaska (U.S.)

Prince William Sound

Canada

NORTH AMERICA

NORTH PACIFIC OCEAN

United States

Hawaiian Is. (U.S.)

CENTRAL AMERICA

Mexico

Gulf of Mexico

Caribbean Sea

Lake Maracaibo

Puerto Rico

Sargasso Sea

Costa Rica

NORTH ATLANTIC OCEAN

Equator

SOUTH PACIFIC OCEAN

Peru

Chile

SOUTH AMERICA

Brazil

ATLANTIC OCEAN

SOUTH ATLANTIC OCEAN

Iceland

Denmark

Norway

Netherlands

Faeroe Is. (Den.)

North Sea

Scotland

Great Britain

France

Spain

Portugal

Gibraltar

EUROPE

Sweden

Baltic Sea

Italy

Greece

Black Sea

Mediterranean Sea

ASIA

Iraq

Kuwait

Algeria

Egypt

Saudi Arabia

AFRICA

Red Sea

Persian Gulf

Liberia

Nigeria

Kenya

INDIAN OCEAN

Madagascar

South Africa

SOUTHERN OCEAN

ANTARCTICA

Antarctic Circle

CHAPTER TWO

A WATERY WORLD

The oceans are not only very large and very deep, they are also constantly on the move. A fascinating variety of plants and animals —ranging from tiny seaweed to the 150-ton (136-metric-ton) blue whale— inhabit the ocean. The ocean's water and the many creatures that live in it form a wonderfully complex world.

WATER ON THE MOVE

Where does ocean water come from? Oceans receive most of their volume from the world's rivers. Scientists have estimated that rivers carry about 28 trillion gallons (106 trillion liters) of water to the oceans every day. This amount equals the water in more than one billion built-in swimming pools!

Oceans are part of a global system called the **water cycle.** All of the earth's water moves through this cycle day after day. To travel through the cycle, water may change its form and location many times. Let's look at how the water cycle works.

Imagine you are a tiny drop of water floating along the surface of the Indian Ocean. The sun's hot rays warm you, and eventually you **evaporate** into the air as water vapor. You float upward, joining other drops in a big rain cloud. In time, as the cloud becomes heavy with water, you fall as rain. When you land on the earth, you might hit a lake or tumble downhill

(Left) A tiny orange clown fish nestles safely within the fingerlike tentacles of a giant sea anemone. Used to sting and kill other fish, the tentacles do not harm the clown fish, which attracts the giant anemone's food with its bright color.

to a river that empties into the ocean. Once you reach the ocean again, you have completed the water cycle.

This dizzying trip has many other side visits. You might find yourself caught up in ice, such as in a glacier. You could seep deeply into the ground, becoming groundwater. Some drops are soaked up by the roots of plants. But, like all drops of water, you would eventually find yourself on the

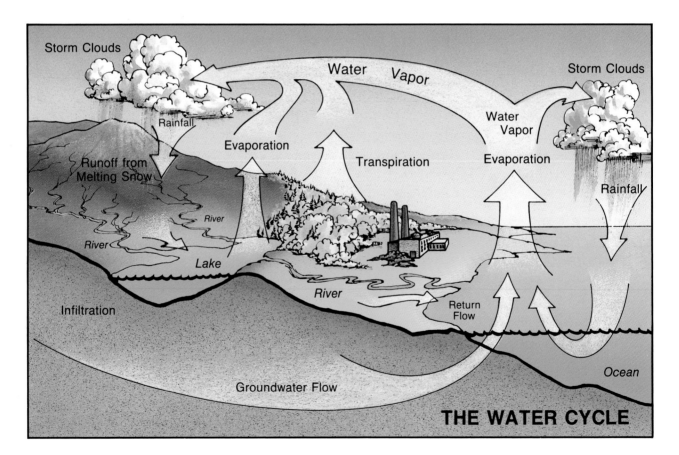

THE WATER CYCLE

move once more, traveling from place to place and from one shape to another in this endless cycle from the ocean and back again.

OCEAN MOTIONS

Our planet is constantly in motion, circling the sun in a yearly journey and turning on its axis in a daily rotation. These earthly movements affect the behavior of the water in oceans. For example, strong winds are created when sunlight heats the air around our planet. These winds drag across the surface of oceans and make the water move.

Winds that blow across the broad expanses of water form waves—the "ocean motion" you probably know best. Maybe you have seen waves pounding against rocks on the shore or gently lapping against the sand. Most ocean waves are 10 to 12 feet (3 to 3.5 meters) high.

Another ocean activity is a **current,** or a movement of the surface water of the ocean. Winds, combined with the rotation

Wearing wet suits to protect them from cold ocean water, three friends dodge incoming waves.

of the earth, cause most currents. The strongest current is found around Antarctica. The Gulf Stream moves between Europe and North America. In the Indian Ocean, powerful winds—called monsoons—change the direction of regional currents twice a year.

Currents help to distribute warmth and coolness around the earth. They push warm water from the **tropics** (the region that encircles the equator) northward to cooler areas. For example, the Gulf Stream brings water with higher temperatures to Iceland. The water warms the air around this North Atlantic island, making Reykjavík, the country's capital, warmer than New York City, which lies far to the south!

Despite its name, Iceland—an island in the far north of our planet—has a fairly mild climate. The Gulf Stream Current brings warm tropical air to Iceland, making it possible for Icelanders to enjoy many outdoor activities.

UPS AND DOWNS

Tides are another "moving experience" for ocean water. On a typical seashore, say at Australia's Bondi Beach, the edge of the water moves in close to shore and then out toward the horizon twice a day. This movement is caused by the gravitational tug of the moon and the sun on the earth. The tug makes the water in the ocean rise and then fall away from the coast about every 12 hours.

Young Mexicans wait onshore as waves come in at high tide.

During the course of a day, as the earth spins, different shores take turns being near or far from the moon. When a shore is directly in line with the moon's gravitational pull, the water rises and rushes inland, making **high tide.** When a shore is out of line with the moon's pull, the strength of the tug decreases, and the water moves out to sea at **low tide.**

Tidal waves, despite their name, have nothing to do with the tide. Instead, they are a natural reaction of ocean water to earthquakes, volcanoes, and other sudden movements beneath the ocean. These motions set up huge shudders that create very

At low tide, boats are stranded in the harbor of a small fishing village in northwestern France.

A giant wave called a tsunami crashed into Lisbon, Portugal, in 1755, destroying most of this European city.

long waves. The waves can travel up to 500 miles (800 kilometers) per hour in the water.

The resulting waves—today more commonly known as **tsunamis**—may be barely noticeable in the open sea, where no land breaks the ocean's surface. As the waves approach land, however, the rising ground pushes up a tall wall of water that can reach as much as 130 feet (40 meters) in height. Entire cities and villages have been washed away by tsunamis.

Lisbon, the capital of Portugal, was leveled in 1755 when 50-foot (15-meter) waves hit the country's Atlantic coast during a tsunami. In 1946, the Hawaiian Islands in the Pacific Ocean got the full force of a series of tsunamis caused by earthquakes off the coast of Alaska.

AN UNDERSEA WEB

Within all this busy, moving water is a fascinating world of plants and animals. From the waves to the seafloor, the oceans are layered with life. Tiny plants and animals called **plankton** float near the surface. Fish and other animals glide through the various depths of the sea.

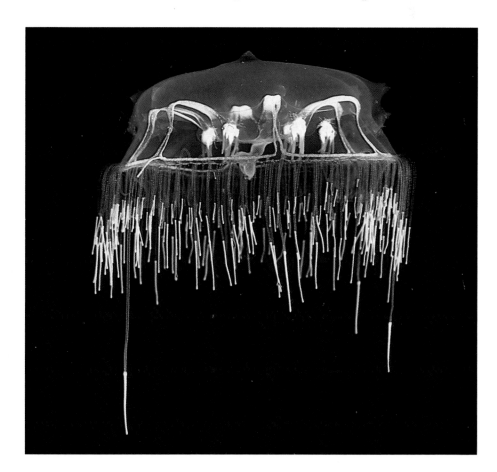

Although it looks like a jellyfish, this animal is a type of zooplankton known as Halicreas minimum. *As it floats and drifts through the ocean, the Halicreas uses its tentacles to trap and kill its prey.*

Some live near the brightly lit surface. Others inhabit a twilight area where a little bit of sunlight reaches the undersea world. Still other sea animals survive in the eternal darkness of the deep, deep ocean.

All of these plants and animals are linked together in a complex system called a **food web.** It involves tiny creatures that become the food source for other animals, who in turn are the food source for still other, usually larger creatures. This meals-in-a-row plan makes the ocean a living restaurant!

At one end of the chain are hard-to-see **phytoplankton** (meaning "plant floaters") and seaweeds that use the sun's heat energy to grow. **Zooplankton** (animal floaters) feed on the phytoplankton. Shrimp eat the zooplankton and are then consumed by fish. Tiny **krill** (shrimplike animals) are food for seals, squid, and whales. Most fish simply eat other fish and then become a meal for yet another **species** (kind) of fish. The entire, complex system allows plants and animals to thrive, reproduce, and die in a natural, balanced way.

CORAL REEFS
Loved to Death

Colorful fish inhabit a coral reef near the Hawaiian Islands.

Found only in warm, shallow tropical waters, coral reefs are among the world's most beautiful marine (sea-based) habitats. Hardened masses of orange, yellow, red, and purple corals make splashes of color in shapes that look like fans, mushrooms, and lettuce leaves. Other animals—such as sea urchins and **sea anemones**—dwell in the nooks and crannies of the reefs.

These underwater gardens, which build up over thousands of years, are very easy to destroy. At the bottom of a coral reef are the limestone skeletons of tiny dead animals, called corals. Individual living corals, known as **polyps,** anchor their tubelike bodies to the dead corals. As polyps eat phytoplankton, reproduce, and die, they add their skeletons to the existing reef. Over time, a reef can grow quite big. The Great Barrier Reef, which is located off the northeastern coast of Australia, is more than 1,000 miles (1,609 kilometers) long.

Because coral reefs often lie near seashores, they are fairly easy for us to reach. As a result, in places like Florida, Hawaii, and Australia, these reefs are in danger of being over-visited or loved to death. Reef walking—strolling across the top of hardened coral at low tide—can damage a coral reef if a walker's actions disturb polyps. Cruise boats bump against reefs to drop off scuba divers. Vacationers carelessly maneuver their fishing vessels into the fragile reef environment.

Although all of these human actions harm coral reefs, the biggest people-made problem comes from the pollution of the water in which coral reefs form. Unless we stop putting sewage, garbage, and poisonous chemicals in the ocean, reefs may not survive, even if we learn to watch our step.

CHAPTER THREE

PEOPLE AND OCEANS

Half of the five billion people on our planet live along or near the ocean. We build homes and port cities along seacoasts because we depend on the sea for many important things in our everyday lives. Let's look at some of the ways we use oceans.

OCEAN RICHES

Have you ever had a tuna sandwich or fish and chips? If you have, you have taken part in one of humankind's oldest activities— gathering food from the sea. Scientists have found evidence that 10,000 years ago people in Europe caught fish from the North Sea. In modern times, the ocean still provides a rich harvest. In fact, fish are the main food for people in many countries around the world.

(Left) The Canadian port city of Vancouver, British Columbia, has grown and prospered because of its location on the North Pacific Ocean. (Above) Workers in a factory in Peru, South America, pack cans of freshly caught tuna.

Oceans provide us with many valuable products, including seafood for our tables (left) and pearls used in making jewelry (above).

Roughly 12 million people make a living by fishing. The main fish-catching countries are Japan, Russia, China, the United States, Chile, Norway, India, South Korea, Thailand, and Indonesia. Oceans offer many other goods besides seafood. Pearls,

Saudi Arabia, a desert nation in the Middle East, lacks plentiful sources of fresh water. The country has built many coastal desalination plants—factories that make fresh water by taking the salt out of seawater.

natural sponges, and seaweed help us make items ranging from expensive jewelry to valuable medicines.

Fresh water is another important thing people get from the ocean. Scientists have invented special factories, called **desalination plants,** to remove the salt from ocean water. The resulting fresh water—which humans need to survive—can be used for drinking, for cooking, and for irrigating farmland.

People in places like Saudi Arabia, Mexico, and the Netherlands depend on water from the ocean for their fresh water. Countries throughout the world produce about

1.25 billion gallons (4.7 billion liters) of fresh water from salt water every day.

MINING THE SEA

Ocean water holds various minerals, including the ordinary seasoning called salt. In ancient times, people from China, Egypt, Greece, and Italy got salt from the sea and used it to flavor and preserve food. China, France, India, Japan, and Spain still produce salt by letting seawater evaporate until just salt is left.

About half of the world's magnesium comes from seawater. This mineral—a necessary part of aircraft engines, rockets, missiles, and cameras—is also vital to human life. Bromine, which is used in photography, medicines, and gasoline, is another valuable mineral found in salt water.

The floor of the ocean is rich in sulfur, phosphorus, limestone, and other minerals. Perhaps the most visible sign of our use of the ocean floor is an **offshore well.** Workers have drilled these wells into the seabed to tap oil and natural gas. Nearly

This offshore well near western Australia drills for natural gas beneath the floor of the Indian Ocean.

one-fourth of all the world's oil and natural gas comes from offshore sites.

Drilling platforms currently dot the Black Sea in eastern Europe, the Gulf of Mexico, the Arctic Ocean, and the North Sea. Wells also exist in the Sulu Sea in eastern Asia, the North Pacific Ocean, and Lake Maracaibo in northern South America.

Humans have long traveled on the oceans. In the eighth century, Viking ships (left) journeyed from Norway, Sweden, and Denmark to raid other parts of Europe. This modern cargo vessel (above) steams through the waters of the Persian Gulf to reach the Indian Ocean.

ACROSS THE WAVES

We also use oceans as highways. Thousands of years ago, Asian people traveled on rafts and in dugout canoes to settle the tiny islands that dot the South Pacific Ocean.

The ancient Arabs crossed the Indian Ocean to trade goods with people in Africa and India. Christopher Columbus and other European explorers took to the seas to chart new lands and to search for wealth.

Transport by ocean is still a common and cheap way of carrying goods to market. Large ships called tankers move thousands of tons of oil to distant harbors. Ports throughout the world—including Rotterdam in the Netherlands, Tokyo in Japan, and Vancouver in Canada—welcome cargo vessels from many different nations.

TAPPING OCEAN ENERGY

Our constantly moving oceans have long provided energy to meet human needs. Ancient Egyptians used the strength of tides to run simple machinery. In the eleventh century, tidal power operated mills that ground grain in Great Britain.

Factories in China, France, Great Britain, Canada, and Russia now make electricity using tidal energy. The largest tidal facility operates in France on the

High tides bring water into this energy station in northern France. At low tide, the stored water is released in a steady, downward stream to run machinery that produces electricity.

Rance River, which flows into a channel of the Atlantic Ocean. The plant produces 608 million kilowatts of energy per year. This is enough power to operate more than 600,000 color television sets, 24 hours a day, for a year.

SCUBA DIVING
The Great Underwater Adventure

Every deep-sea diver owes thanks to Jacques Cousteau and Emile Gagnan. In the 1940s, they invented the Aqua-lung—a device that enables swimmers to breathe under water and to move freely at the same time. The sport that resulted from this invention—called scuba diving—has attracted many fans. The word *scuba* stands for *Self-Contained Underwater Breathing Apparatus*.

In many underwater operations, sophisticated scuba gear is now standard equipment. It consists of a face mask, a snorkel, an air tank, an air hose, an air regulator, a pressure gauge, fins, and a weight belt. These items are worn over a wet suit and a flotation vest. A diver might also wear other items, but these are the basic pieces of equipment.

The glass face mask allows a diver to see well under water, and the snorkel (a short tube) can be used to breathe at the surface. Fins permit a swimmer to move with ease, and the weight belt helps a diver to sink. The foam-rubber wet suit keeps a diver warm in cold water, and the vest can be inflated to bring a diver to the surface in a hurry.

The tank, hose, and regulator, which work as a unit, are designed like the Cousteau-Gagnan Aqua-lung. The tank's air is compressed, meaning it has been pumped under pressure into the container. A diver breathes through the hose that is attached to the tank, and the regulator controls the flow of air. The pressure gauge tells the diver how much air is left in the tank.

Fin

Knife

Snorkel

Air tank

Face mask

Air regulator

Wet suit

Air hose

Pressure gauge

Floatation vest

Weight belt

Scientists are also investigating the energy of ocean waves as a nonpolluting fuel source. In Algeria, researchers are testing a device that uses waves to create electricity. Wave-powered generators already operate in Norway. When navigators bring their ships near Japan, lighthouses that run on wave energy guide the vessels to safety.

SPLASHING AND TRASHING

The ocean is important as a source of fun, too. People sail their own boats or take pleasure cruises across the sparkling waters. Scuba divers, swimmers, and surfers splash in the waves. Many people travel to sandy beaches to bask in the warm sun. Others collect shells that wash ashore.

Another big use we humans have for the ocean is as a global trash can. In the same way you might take out your family's garbage, many countries "take out" their garbage to the ocean. Much of this global trash does not disappear. Instead, it fouls the habitats of many marine (sea-based) animals and plants.

A merchant vessel dumps its cargo—waste from the mining of jarosite, a yellowish brown mineral—into the ocean near Australia.

(Right) *In another part of Australia, a diver explores the wonders of the Great Barrier Reef. (Below) A brother and sister lay the foundation for a sand castle on a beach in South Carolina.*

CHAPTER FOUR

OUR ENDANGERED OCEANS

Dolphins—among the smartest sea mammals—die in nets set by tuna fishermen in the Pacific Ocean. Coastal cities in the United States dump millions of gallons of garbage and toxic (poisonous) chemicals into the sea every day. People in Southeast Asia dynamite life-rich coral reefs in Indonesia to capture fish that end up in salt-water aquariums. Trawlers (boats that drag nets) in the North Sea catch more herring in one season than can be replaced by the hatch of new fish. Drilling platforms off the coast of northern South America put a greasy film of oil on the surface of Lake Maracaibo.

From the Arctic to the Southern, from the Pacific to the Atlantic, people's actions are endangering the ocean. We are not just using the ocean gently and wisely to tap its resources. Rather, we are carelessly

(Left) Garbage that has washed ashore from ocean dumping litters Gibraltar, a British-held peninsula in the southern part of Spain. (Above) Oil derricks that support drilling equipment dot the surface of Venezuela's Lake Maracaibo, an inlet of the Caribbean Sea.

To capture fish, this stern trawler tows a wide-mouthed net—called an otter trawl—along the seafloor.

making the ocean meet our needs without looking at the results—both now and in the future.

A FINE KETTLE OF FISH

A hundred years ago, people harvested the ocean's riches carefully. For example, people often used hooks and bait or small nets to catch only the fish they needed to feed their families. Crews from fishing villages also worked during specific seasons, avoiding certain species at breeding times. These methods meant popular species would survive and reproduce so that there would be plenty of fish in seasons to come.

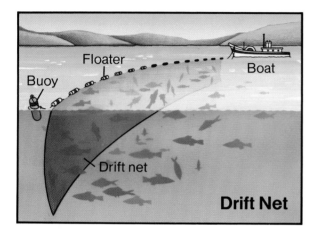

When hung in the water from a boat, a drift net (top) forms a curtain that entangles fish that swim into it. Although designed to catch herring and salmon, drift nets also trap dolphins (bottom).

Such long-term fishing methods are not widely practiced today. For example, many fishing boats set huge **drift nets,** which can reach 100 feet (30 meters) deep and 50 miles (80 kilometers) wide. These traps catch everything that gets in their way—from herring to dolphins. In the Pacific Ocean alone, 30,000 miles (48,279 kilometers) of drift nets are in operation every night. If all these nets were connected, they would encircle the earth!

Forty years ago, the worldwide salt-water catch was about 23 million tons (21 million metric tons) per year. Because of changes in technology, that annual total had jumped to 93 million tons (84 million metric tons) by the late 1980s. International experts predict that in the year 2000, we will be hauling in up to 165 million tons (150 million metric tons) of seafood.

In some cases, the numbers we catch are so high that there are too few fish left to breed to replace them. This development is called **overfishing** and has resulted in the decline of many species, including herring, albacore tuna, and haddock.

AQUACULTURE
Down on the Fish Farm

Aquaculture—the raising of animals and plants that live in water —is an age-old method of providing food. In modern times, most aquaculture takes place in tanks, in cages, or on rafts. Fish lay their eggs in these pens. After hatching, the babies are cared for until they are large enough to be harvested.

Trout, salmon, clams, oysters, and lobster are some of the main aquacultural crops. Japanese and Chinese aquaculturists grow large amounts of seaweed and shellfish every year. Trout come from U.S. fish farms. Three-fourths of Ecuador's shrimp harvest is the result of aquaculture.

Workers on an aquacultural farm in Malaysia inspect the tanks of growing fish.

Since the early 1970s, the aquacultural industry has introduced new high-tech equipment. Computers monitor the temperature in some tanks, and robots feed the growing fish.

These changes have helped to make aquaculture the source of 10 percent of the world's entire catch of fish. Experts think this percentage will go up as our population increases and creates a greater demand for seafood.

Aquaculture may also help us to solve the problem of overfishing by giving ocean fish a chance to rebuild their numbers in their natural salt-water habitats.

CARELESS DUMPING

For centuries, we have dumped our garbage into the big, seemingly endless ocean, pretending that the trash will disappear. As our world's population has grown larger, the amount of dumping has also increased.

Most of the waste people put into the oceans is either **sewage sludge,** the solids left over after treatment plants have cleaned sewer water, or **dredge spoil.** This is material dug up from harbors and other shallow areas when we deepen sea-lanes.

Each year, the United States alone releases 9 million tons (8 million metric tons) of sewage sludge and 198 million tons (180 million metric tons) of dredge spoil into the Atlantic and Pacific oceans. We would need more than 100 million pickup trucks to move this much dirt. The polluted waters

A boat near France releases its load of sludge as it sails.

surrounding New York City lie above nearly 100 feet (30 meters) of dredge spoil and sewage sludge.

In many countries, **raw sewage**—the liquid waste from drains, toilets, and sewers—empties right into the ocean. Raw sewage is completely untreated, meaning no effort has been made to remove disease-causing life forms, human waste, and other polluting materials. In the 1980s, 90 percent of the sewage that went into the Mediterranean Sea was untreated.

We use the ocean as a giant dumpster for other types of garbage, too. Barges transport urban trash to deep-sea locations, where it is shoved overboard. Oceangoing vessels have long unloaded their sewage as they sail. In an average day, cruise ships release five and a half million metal, glass, and plastic objects into the ocean while their passengers suntan and swim.

Factories in rich nations often put toxic chemicals into the ocean, too. The United States, for example, has two ocean sites just for getting rid of the waste produced by various industries. Great Britain dumps

Cruise ships, as well as military vessels, routinely dump their garbage overboard as they travel to distant ports.

much of its toxic waste into the North Sea.

Nuclear wastes—most of which come from factories that make weapons and nuclear energy—also have found their way into the sea. Between 1946 and 1970, the United States sank 90,000 drums of nuclear waste at six sites in the Pacific and Atlantic oceans. Similarly, the British and Dutch dumped their nuclear wastes into the Atlantic Ocean off the coast of Spain. Naval accidents have left nuclear weapons and nuclear equipment on the ocean floor.

OILING THE OCEAN

Oil and its by-products fuel our cars, factories, and furnaces. In our hurry to tap oil, we have oiled the ocean, too. Disastrous oil spills have been in the news in the past few years. The 1989 leakage from the *Exxon Valdez*, an oil tanker that ran aground off Alaska's coast, is an example of an oil spill. Other serious releases of oil occurred off the coast of the Middle East in 1991 and in the North Sea in 1993.

In past decades, the United States frequently put drums filled with dangerous nuclear waste into the ocean. Although the practice stopped in 1983, the drums are still on the ocean floor.

Oil is especially damaging because it floats on the surface of the water and travels long distances. The greasy liquid coats everything in its path with heavy, sticky chemicals.

Spills put a large amount of oil into a single spot at one time and can happen in many ways. Some spills occur when oil wells leak. In 1979, for example, an oil well off the coast of Mexico accidentally blew up, pouring millions of gallons of oil into the Gulf of Mexico. Other spills are a result of accidents involving the ships that carry oil. Throughout the world, thousands of oil spills occur each year.

Many people mistake these spills as the source of most of the ocean's oil problems. In the 1980s, spills accounted for only about 600,000 barrels out of the millions of barrels of oil that went into the ocean each year. The rest came from less obvious activities.

A well in the Campeche oil field in the Gulf of Mexico blew up in 1979 and took nearly a year to plug. The resulting oil slick killed many kinds of wildlife living in the gulf.

At a shipyard in South Carolina, a cargo vessel washes out its oil tanks, putting the oiled waste into coastal waters.

Oil enters the ocean when factories drain their used water, when ships wash out their tanks, and when water runs off city streets. Home mechanics dump 11 million gallons (42 million liters) of used car oil down the drain every two and a half weeks.

SOMETHING IN THE AIR

Air is part of the water cycle. Droplets of water travel through the air when they are drawn upward to the clouds as water vapor. Eventually, the drops travel back to earth in the form of rain or snow. But what happens when the air is polluted? You guessed it, the droplets also become polluted. As a result, oceans get a taste of this global problem, too.

For example, factories, power plants, and cars put lots of carbon dioxide (CO_2) into the air through their smokestacks and exhaust systems. Small amounts of this

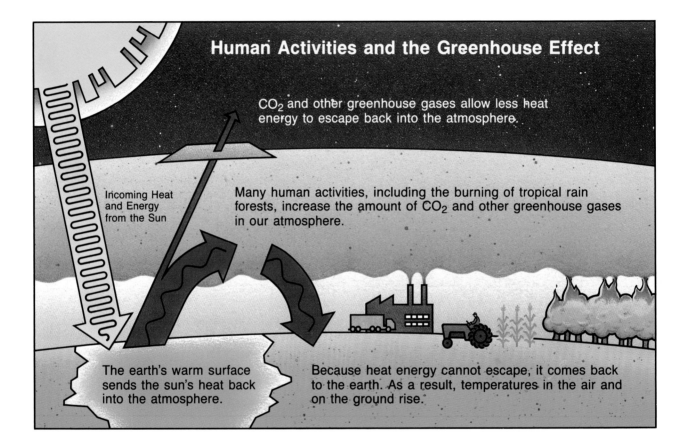

Human Activities and the Greenhouse Effect

CO_2 and other greenhouse gases allow less heat energy to escape back into the atmosphere.

Incoming Heat and Energy from the Sun

Many human activities, including the burning of tropical rain forests, increase the amount of CO_2 and other greenhouse gases in our atmosphere.

The earth's warm surface sends the sun's heat back into the atmosphere.

Because heat energy cannot escape, it comes back to the earth. As a result, temperatures in the air and on the ground rise.

odorless and colorless gas are a natural part of our atmosphere. But cars and factories put more and more CO_2 into the air every year, and large amounts of the gas are collecting in our planet's atmosphere.

Some scientists believe that increased amounts of CO_2 will raise the earth's temperature. Like the roof of a glass greenhouse, CO_2 lets in sunlight but traps the sun's heat that tries to return to the atmosphere. This process is sometimes called the **greenhouse effect.**

If the amount of trapped CO_2 continues to rise, so will global temperatures. The earth and its oceans may warm up. At higher global temperatures, ice caps could melt and add more water to the oceans. Sea levels might rise, flooding coastal cities. Global warming could also affect ocean currents, which play a major role in our planet's weather.

Other chemicals and gases—including deadly pollutants called hazardous wastes —are released into the ocean every year. Near the North Sea, for example, about 100,000 tons (90,720 metric tons) of hazardous wastes are burned annually. These bonfires release toxic gases and chemicals into the air and water.

Another group of chemical pollutants, called **chloro-fluoro-carbons (CFCs),** are causing problems in our atmosphere that could affect the ocean. **Ozone** is a gas that forms a fragile, natural shield high above the earth's surface. This gas filters out harmful rays from the sun. In 1974,

scientists discovered that CFCs were drifting upward into the ozone and weakening the shield.

As the ozone layer thins, more harmful rays reach our planet. Experts predict that marine life—particularly the phytoplankton at the base of the food web—may be damaged if our ozone layer becomes too thin. Around Antarctica, where the ozone layer is weak, some destruction has already taken place.

The purple splotch on this computer map of Antarctica shows where our planet's protective shield, called the ozone layer, is dangerously thin. The ocean's plants and animals are particularly sensitive to harmful rays from the sun that now can pass through the thinning ozone layer.

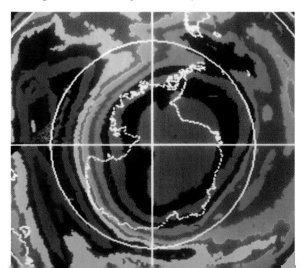

CHAPTER FIVE

LIVING WITH OUR MISTAKES

Throughout the last few decades, people's actions have affected the health of the ocean. For example, we catch fish by the megaton. Barges piled with trash and drums full of toxic chemicals end up in the ocean. We foul the rivers that lead to the ocean. Do all these actions really make a difference to something so big and deep? The answer, of course, is YES.

A century and a half ago, when the world's population was much smaller, human actions had only a minor effect on oceans. These huge, salty bodies of water were big enough to handle small amounts of garbage and waste. The damage of our actions was reversible, meaning the oceans would eventually return to the way they were before the damage happened.

But today the world's population is five times as large as it was 150 years ago. The number of factories has also grown, and we have added cars to the equation, too. As a result of our growth, we have begun to harm the ocean in ways that are not reversible. Let's look at the long-term effects of our recent actions on the oceans.

FADED FISHING

Every year, commercial fishing boats haul in more fish to feed our growing population. Large catches would not be a problem if the fish that were left could lay their eggs fast enough to keep up with us. But by

(Left) Sea turtles often drown when they become tangled in nets and other fishing gear that have been thrown away or lost. Most of the world's species of sea turtles are endangered by human actions.

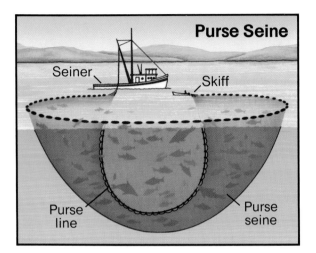

Purse Seine

Purse seines allow fishing crews to catch huge groups, or schools, of fish. A boat called a seiner drops the purse seine, which a faster boat known as a skiff drags around the school. When the ends of the trap join, the bottom closes, capturing everything inside the net.

overfishing we are taking fish faster than they can reproduce. Specialists say that if we want to reverse this trend, we must limit the annual world catch to 26 million tons (24 million metric tons). This is one-third of what we are pulling in now!

Other experts tell us that more than 40 species of fish are in danger of disappearing because of overfishing. Species that have been overfished include haddock off the eastern coast of the United States and herring in the seas near northern Europe.

The situation of the anchovy is a good example of what overfishing can do. Since the early 1950s, fishing crews from Peru in South America have caught billions of these tiny fish to sell to other countries. Most of the anchovies are ground up as food for livestock. In 1970, anchovies were Peru's number-one export, with more than 13 million tons (12 million metric tons) of anchovies caught in a single year!

Experts worried that the anchovies were overfished, but Peruvian fishery officials did not listen to suggestions of limiting the annual anchovy catch. By 1980, Peruvian fishing crews could find only 793,656 tons (720,000 metric tons) of anchovies.

Some people blamed the loss on El Niño, a warm ocean current that occasionally occurs along the South American coast. But most experts believe overfishing decreased the anchovy hauls and hurt Peru's economy.

Changes in the technology of fishing have also affected marine creatures. Fishing crews from Japan, South Korea, and Taiwan use drift nets to catch squid to sell in global markets. These huge nets are left alone for days. Meanwhile, trapped seabirds, turtles, whales, and dolphins die in the nets. Up to 100,000 dolphins and 800,000 seabirds are killed annually in drift nets.

Dolphins often swim near large groups of tuna. Many tuna-catching crews drop their **purse seines** (round nets) when they see dolphins break the surface of the ocean. In the 1970s, nearly 200,000 dolphins died in these traps each year. People objected to this fishing practice by refusing to buy tuna and by writing letters of protest to tuna-canning companies. By the early 1990s, some companies had stopped or limited this harmful fishing method and had begun to market their products as "dolphin safe."

BELLY UP IN THE BAY

In 1987, 750 dead dolphins washed ashore in North Carolina and New Jersey. The killers of these sea mammals were people-

Workers use a stretcher to return a rescued dolphin to its ocean habitat. Many stranded dolphins are not so lucky. Others wash ashore, too sick from polluted ocean water to survive.

made poisons, such as **poly-chlorinated biphenyls (PCBs).** These chemicals entered the ocean and became part of the food web. When the dolphins fed on poisoned fish, they also ate the poisons.

More examples of marine die-offs exist. The number of striped bass in the Atlantic Ocean is the lowest in 25 years. Scientists blame this situation on PCBs and other chemical pollutants that weaken the

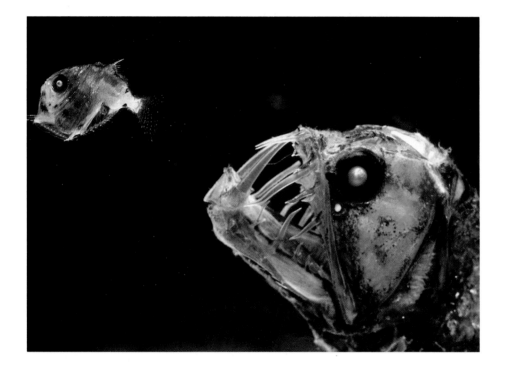

A viperfish sneaks up on its next meal. When large fish eat smaller polluted fish, the big fish get the pollution, too. We become part of this process, called bioaccumulation, when we eat diseased fish.

young bass and kill their eggs. Fish full of PCBs and another poisonous chemical known as DDT are food for seals in the Baltic Sea, which lies south and east of Sweden. As a result of PCBs, populations of Baltic seals have dropped drastically. Some scientists estimate that at least three-quarters of the Baltic's female seals may be unable to have pups because of PCBs.

The reason so many creatures can die from poisoning is **bioaccumulation,** a process that occurs when an animal gradually absorbs and stores a chemical in its body. When the animal is eaten, it passes the chemical up the food web.

For example, plankton take in tiny amounts of pollutants, which the fish that consume plankton then absorb. Because the plankton-eaters feed on lots of plankton during their lifetimes, they store more pollutants than a single plankton does. Animals that swallow the plankton-eaters end up with even higher amounts of the pollutant inside them. By the time dolphins, seals, and other large animals enter the food web by eating fish, the amount of a specific pollutant in a particular fish may be fatal.

Dolphins and seals are not the only animals that eat contaminated fish. Humans dine on fish, too. People in Europe and North America have been warned against consuming too many fish and shellfish from polluted ocean waters.

Health officials in New York State, for example, recommend that, because of contamination, people eat fish caught in the nearby ocean no more than once a week. Some scientists in Peru traced a 1991 outbreak of the disease cholera to the polluted fish that people bought from local vendors along the Pacific coast. In Japan in the 1950s, more than 600 people died from eating tainted fish.

A TANGLED TALE

Of all the trash that reaches the sea, things made of plastic cause some of the worst problems. Old fishing nets, six-pack beverage rings, and plastic bags kill hundreds of thousands of marine animals and birds each year. These creatures mistake the plastics for food or toys and eat or get tangled up in them.

A discarded plastic six-pack ring is cutting into the neck of this sea lion. If the ring is not removed, the animal could die from suffocation (lack of air).

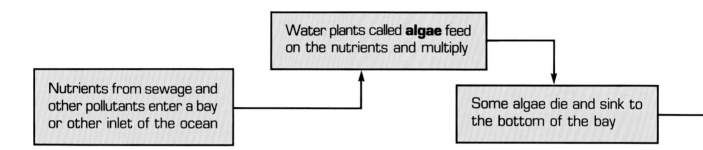

Nutrients from sewage and other pollutants enter a bay or other inlet of the ocean

Water plants called **algae** feed on the nutrients and multiply

Some algae die and sink to the bottom of the bay

Plastics float, making them easy for many animals to reach. Researchers have seen birds trying to feed bits of plastic to their young. Endangered sea turtles gobble up plastic bags and balloons because they look like jellyfish—a key food source. Another endangered species, the humpback whale, is sometimes found tangled in plastic.

TOO RICH

Oceans are rich in many types of animals and plants. But pollutants like sewage bring in other riches called **nutrients** to salt water. These nutrients are the food that plants, including phytoplankton, need to grow. When water plants die, they use up oxygen as they rot. In large amounts, however, nutrients can cause the growth of so much plant material that the water loses lots of oxygen. Since marine animals need oxygen to live, a loss of oxygen in salt water may result in large-scale die-offs.

Low oxygen levels have killed fish near the coasts of Europe, North America, South America, Africa, Asia, and Australia. The dead fish that wash ashore have ruined beaches in Chile, Italy, Nigeria, Pakistan, Russia, and the United States.

Sometimes nutrients cause an even worse problem. They encourage the growth of **toxic algae,** tiny water plants that are poisonous to living things that feed on them.

Tiny life forms called **bacteria** feed on the dead algae

As they feed, the bacteria use up the oxygen in the water

Marine animals need oxygen to live. Oxygen losses cause some fish and shellfish to die or leave the bay

In 1989, toxic algae destroyed all marine life in the top 50 feet (15 meters) of water in the channel that links the North and Baltic seas. Toxic algae have poisoned shellfish off Central America and near the Philippine Islands in Southeast Asia.

A WHALE OF A TIME

You may have heard the cry, "Save the Whales!" In the early 1990s, all nine of the world's great whale species were in danger of becoming **extinct**—that is, of no longer existing. The unchecked killing of whales during the last 100 years accounts for this decline in whale numbers.

For centuries, hunters have valued whales for the oil in their blubber (fat) and for their flesh. At the beginning of the 1900s, the explosive harpoon and other changes in technology made whale hunting more efficient. In the 1930–1931 whaling season, for example, hunters killed 30,000 blue whales in Antarctic waters alone. The total population of this species now numbers only about 10,000 worldwide!

GRACEFUL GIANTS

These bottle-nosed dolphins belong to the toothed group of cetaceans.

Although most ocean dwellers are fish, the largest sea creatures are mammals like us. They are warm blooded, they develop their young within their bodies, and the mothers produce milk to feed the babies. These incredible creatures—members of the mammal group Cetacea—include whales, porpoises, and dolphins.

Cetaceans are divided into two groups—those with teeth and those without teeth. Toothed whales eat fish, squid, or small sea animals. Toothless whales have rows of flexible strips, called **baleen,** in the upper part of their mouths. When these whales gulp water, they use the baleen to filter out krill—their main source of food.

Among toothed cetaceans are sperm whales, beluga whales, and dolphins. Baleen whales include the right, the gray, and the humpback. The largest mammal living on our planet is the krill-eating blue whale. It can weigh as much as 220 tons (200 metric tons)—the same as about 25 elephants. Blue whales can grow to about 100 feet (30 meters) in length (about one-third of a football field).

Cetaceans, like all mammals, need air to breathe. A whale takes in oxygen at the ocean's surface through a nostril in the top of its head. Gracefully arching out of the water, the animal exhales and inhales in about two

A krill-eating humpback whale arches out of the water as it takes a gulp of air.

seconds. This one breath will allow a cetacean to stay under water for one to two hours.

Some whales move back and forth between specific areas of the ocean in different seasons. A female blue whale, for example, may spend the summer near Antarctica in the Southern Ocean and then mate in the fall. She may travel northward to warm waters in the Pacific Ocean to give birth in the winter. The newborn whale, called a calf, usually weighs more than 2 tons (1.8 metric tons) and gains 200 pounds (91 kilograms) a day on its mother's milk. After about seven months, the calf can eat krill and accompanies its mother on the journey back to Antarctica.

Female whales usually have babies once every two years. Because of this slow birth rate, whales have not been able to replace the number killed by hunters. International laws against whale killing are giving these cetaceans a chance to make a comeback.

The butchered carcasses of dead whales line a dock on the Faeroe Islands in the North Atlantic Ocean. Worldwide, only about 100,000 whales—of all species— still survive out of a population that once numbered in the millions.

Similarly, the 7,000 humpback whales that exist today are only a shadow of the more than 100,000 that existed in the early 1900s. At least 100,000 right whales once populated the ocean—a sharp contrast to the 300 left on this planet today.

In 1982, many countries agreed not to hunt whales anymore. Norway, Japan, and Iceland did not join this ban and continued to kill whales commercially or in the name of scientific research. In the early 1990s, these three nations were still hunting whales. Although these huge sea mammals are now safe from most hunters, whales can only survive if their habitat survives. If we continue to poison the ocean, whales may yet become extinct.

SPOILED BY OIL

Oil spills can hurt wildlife in many different ways. For example, oil mats the fur or feathers of some creatures, preventing them from staying warm. Some birds become too sticky and heavy to fly. They thus cannot find their own food or are easy prey for larger creatures.

Oil can also suffocate, poison, or give cancer to sea dwellers. The oil slicks can deform unhatched fish or destroy a local food supply. Moreover, damage from oil does not just happen where the oil is spilled. Oil floats on the water's surface, and currents can carry it far from the site to harm life elsewhere.

In 1989, oil damage was big news in Alaska, when the *Exxon Valdez* accidentally dumped 11 million gallons (42 million liters) of crude oil into the ocean. The slick covered 3,000 square miles (7,800 square kilometers), an area that equals 1,452 football fields.

In 1989, the tanker Exxon Valdez *spilled millions of gallons of oil into Alaska's Prince William Sound. Booms (below right) were set up to entrap some of the oil, while workers (above right) tried to clean the sticky liquid from the area's wildlife, including this blackened cormorant.*

Less than two years later, during the Persian Gulf War, Iraq opened the valves on several Kuwaiti oil-storage units. Bombing raids also damaged a refinery and released additional oil. The world's largest oil spill happened in 1993, when a tanker sank in the North Sea, losing its cargo of 25 million gallons (95 million liters) of oil.

REEF MADNESS

Coral reefs are life-rich undersea communities that exist in warm, shallow salt water. The limestone skeletons of tiny animals called corals build up over time into huge, rocklike reef formations. Large colonies of living corals remain self-supporting as long as the temperature and the amount of sunlight are constant. Brilliantly colored fish and other kinds of marine life share the corals' space.

These unique marine systems have come under attack in recent years. We prize the color and texture of corals in jewelry and other goods, but our purchases encourage

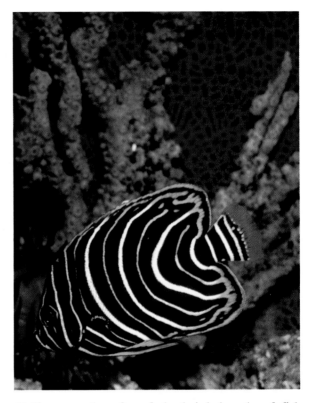

Delicate coral reefs and the brightly colored fish that live in them are easy for us to harm.

the destruction of the reefs. Hunters in Indonesia and Kenya dynamite reefs in search of fish for home salt-water aquariums. Most of the fish are sold to buyers in rich countries. The crews use poisons to stun their prey, killing other species and upsetting the chemical balance of the reef in the process.

Loose soil that rainfall washes into the ocean can also hurt coral reefs. So can dredging, which stirs up tiny particles of dirt that block out the sunlight on which corals depend. Toxic chemicals kill the

Aluminum cans and other garbage line a beach in Atlantic City, New Jersey. Fed up with the ugly litter, people in the state have formed voluntary "trash attacks" to try to clean up some shores.

brightly colored fish and other creatures that live in coral reefs. Some scientists estimate that, unless we change our ways, in 10 years we could lose all of our planet's reefs.

WASTED BEACHES

In the summer of 1988, trash lined the beaches of the eastern United States. Ocean tides and currents brought ashore garbage that had been dumped far out to sea, including medical wastes such as dirty needles and bags of blood. Residents of the East Coast discovered that the mess was both ugly to look at and expensive to clean up.

Many beaches around the world face the same problem. The widespread growth of toxic algae has closed beaches in Italy, Australia, Nigeria, and Chile. In 1989 alone, U.S. volunteers found three million pieces of trash along the seashores. Nearly two-thirds of their catch was plastic, including 467 miles (752 kilometers) of fishing line just in Florida!

CHAPTER SIX

WHAT CAN WE DO?

Because the ocean is so big, it may be easy to think that we cannot make a difference—either to its destruction or to its health. This line of reasoning does not "hold water," meaning it is not true! Dropping a plastic container on the shore is a personal choice. Taking a garbage bag to a beach and collecting discarded aluminum cans and plastic is also an individual action. What each of us does—how we dump our garbage, what we buy, and how we act—can affect oceans.

*(Left) **The cartoon character Popeye warns us about dumping plastic in our oceans.** (Right) **This Florida crew spent a day at the beach—not to suntan and swim but to pick up litter.***

Purse seines often trap dolphins that swim near large schools of tuna. In response to public pressure, some tuna-canning companies have stopped buying or have limited their fish supplies from crews using nets that kill dolphins. To show that they have changed their policy, these companies mark their tuna cans as "dolphin safe."

One thing all of us can do is to tell our leaders that we care about the ocean. When we write letters, or join ocean-protecting organizations, or participate in beach clean-ups, we play an active role in changing the future of oceans.

Rules—especially international ones—protect the ocean from some harmful actions. For example, countries around the world have agreed to ban whale hunting and to avoid dumping industrial waste into the open sea. Because of public protests, some countries have stopped using DDT and CFCs.

Luckily, living by the seashore is not a requirement for working to save our oceans. Here are some suggestions about what all of us can do to be friends of the ocean.

BAGGIN' IT

The last time you visited a beach or a lakeshore, did you notice how much garbage was littering the sand? Well, lots of other folks around the United States have noticed this problem, too! In the past five years, thousands of Americans have volunteered to be part of beach cleanups. Thirty states, plus Puerto Rico and the U.S. Virgin Islands, have annual cleanup programs. Let's take a look at the one in Texas, where the theme is "Don't mess with Texas beaches."

The second largest state, Texas has nearly 400 miles (644 kilometers) of coastline along the Gulf of Mexico. Since 1986, Texans have been traveling to the seashore on a specific day in September to pick up litter. Volunteers have bagged old diapers, empty soft-drink cans, discarded clothing, and plastics in astounding numbers. In 1992, 13,000 Texans collected 172 tons (156 metric tons) of garbage from 163 miles (262 kilometers) of coastline.

In addition to picking up the litter, the volunteers made notes about the garbage so people who enforce the laws that protect marine life will know if the rules are working. The data from beach cleanup programs around the United States have revealed that plastics are the most common danger to ocean life.

Many states have organized cleanup programs on specific days. But we can bring a bag to the seashore any day. As people are saying from Delaware to Hawaii, "Get the Drift and Bag It!"

Volunteers in Texas brave coastal winds to bag ocean trash.

CREATE LESS LITTER. Have a contest with yourself or with a friend to reduce trash. When you purchase something small, for example, avoid taking it from the store in a plastic bag. By making less garbage, we lessen the amount of trash that we dump in oceans.

REUSE, RECYCLE, DO WITHOUT. Recycle everything you can—glass, newspapers, aluminum cans, cardboard, and plastic. If your school does not have a recycling program, ask a parent or teacher to help you start one. Urge your parents to buy products that can be recycled.

MAKE BEACH CLEANUP A GROUP PROJECT. With your family, friends, or classmates, spend a day at the seashore collecting trash and disposing of it properly. Let your mayor or other government person know what and how much you have found. If you do not live near a seashore, clean up a nearby river or lake and you will be doing the ocean a favor, too.

ENCOURAGE YOUR PARENTS TO BUY FROM COMPANIES THAT CARE FOR THE OCEAN. Has an oil corporation polluted the sea through carelessness? Do some tuna companies catch their fish dangerously or wastefully? The way your family spends its money can have an impact on these companies. For example, look for tuna products that are dolphin

safe. Write letters to careless companies telling them why you are not their customer any more.

BE ON THE LOOKOUT FOR WAYS TO AVOID PLASTIC. Choose paper containers whenever possible. Buy soft drinks that come in returnable bottles or in cans stored in cardboard boxes instead of in plastic-ringed six-packs. Cut up six-pack rings so animals will not be able to get their heads caught in the openings. Ask the folks at your fast-food restaurant to wrap your cheeseburger in paper instead of putting it in plastic. Convince your parents to store leftovers in reusable containers rather than in throw-away plastic wrap.

WALK, RIDE YOUR BIKE, TAKE A BUS. These may seem like odd ways to save the ocean, but every time we travel without using a car, we cut down on the demand for oil. This means we help to reduce the chance that oil will pollute the sea. In addition, our nonpolluting modes of transportation lessen the amount of CO_2 that goes into the air.

LEARN ABOUT THE SEA AND ITS CREATURES. Teach your friends and family about the wonders of the ocean—its fish, its movements, and its uses. Encourage people to understand that these vast bodies of water need our attention now so we can enjoy them in the future.

Recycling all possible products—aluminum, newspaper, glass, and plastic—prevents these materials from being dumped in our oceans.

ORGANIZATIONS

CENTER FOR MARINE CONSERVATION
1725 DeSales Street NW, Suite 500
Washington, D.C. 20036

COASTAL CONSERVATION ASSOCIATION
4801 Woodway, Suite 220 West
Houston, Texas 77056

FRIENDS OF THE EARTH
218 D Street SE
Washington, D.C. 20003

GREENPEACE USA
1436 U Street NW
Washington, D.C. 20009

PACIFIC WHALE FOUNDATION
101 North Kihei Road
Kihei, Hawaii 96753

WATER POLLUTION CONTROL FEDERATION
601 Wythe Street
Alexandria, Virginia 22314

Photo Acknowledgments

Photos are used courtesy of: pp. 1, 11 (left), © Stan Osolinski/Root Resources; p. 4, NASA; pp. 6, 36, 40, © David Falconer; pp. 7, 44, Pamela Blades-Eckelbarger, Harbor Branch Oceanographic Institution, Inc.; p. 8 (left), Alton Halverson; p. 8 (right), British Tourist Authority; p. 9, Phil Porter; p. 10, © Mats Wibe Lund/Gardar Pálsson; p. 11 (right), Drs. A. A. M. van der Heyden, Naarden, the Netherlands; pp. 14, 33 (top), John Clifton; p. 17, © Shmuel Thaler; p. 18, Iceland Tourist Board; p. 19 (left), David Mangurian; pp. 19 (right), 24, © Jerg Kroener; p. 20, Mansell Collection. pp. 22–23, 58, © Alex Kerstitch; p. 25, Inter-American Development Bank; p. 26, FAO; p. 27, ARAMCO; p. 28, Australian Information Service; p. 29 (left), Irish Tourist Board, Dublin; p. 29 (right), Embassy of the Islamic Republic of Iran, Ottawa; p. 30, EDF/Sodel; pp. 32–33, © Hewetson/Greenpeace; p. 33 (bottom), South Carolina Land Resources Commission; p. 34, © Midgley/Greenpeace; pp. 35, 62, Independent Picture Service; p. 37 (bottom), © Cannon/Greenpeace; p. 38, Robert Francis/The Hutchison Library; pp. 39, 41, © Gleizes/Greenpeace; p. 42, American Petroleum Institute; p. 43, South Carolina Department of Parks, Recreation, and Tourism; p. 45, NASA/Goddard Space Flight Center; pp. 46, 60, Center for Marine Conservation; p. 49, Marine Mammal Stranding Center; p. 50, © Norbert Wu; p. 51, Sea Shepherd Conservation Society; p. 54, George Grall/National Aquarium in Baltimore; p. 55, © Greenpeace; p. 56, Ros Reeve/The Hutchison Library; p. 57 (top and bottom), © Gary Braasch; p. 59, © Trembley/Greenpeace; p. 61, Heidi B. Lovett/Center for Marine Conservation; p. 63, © Andrew Hammar; pp. 64–65, Jerry Boucher; p. 67, Georgia Department of Natural Resources; p. 68, Marsh Youngbluth, Harbor Branch Oceanographic Institution, Inc.; p. 69, Royal Norwegian Embassy. Charts and illustrations by: pp. 12–13, 31, 37 (top), 44, 48, 53, Laura Westlund; p. 16, Bryan Liedahl.

Front cover: © Elizabeth Simms/Root Resources
Back cover: (left) SATOUR; (right) U.S. Fish and Wildlife, Donald White

algae (AL-jee): small, rootless plants that live in water.

aquaculture (AK-wah-kul-chur): the controlled raising of animals and plants in water to provide food.

bacteria (bak-TEER-i-yah): groups of very small organisms (micro-organisms) that eat living and dead materials.

baleen: the rows of thin, flexible strips in the jaw of a toothless whale that allow it to sift small fish out of seawater.

A young black right whale, also called a cetacean, shows the white underside of its body in the waters off the coast of Georgia.

bioaccumulation (by-o-uh-kew-mew-LAY-shun): the buildup over time of harmful substances in the tissues of animals and plants. These substances can then be passed up to animals and plants higher in the food web.

cetacean (sih-TAY-shun): a member of the mammal group Cetacea that lives in water and has a fishlike body.

channel: a narrow stretch of sea between two land masses that links two larger bodies of water.

chloro-fluoro-carbons (CFCs): chemicals made up of chlorine, fluorine, and carbon that have many industrial uses.

current: the steady movement of the surface water of the ocean in a certain direction.

desalination (dee-sal-ih-NAY-shun) plant: a factory that removes salt from salt water to make fresh water.

dredge spoil: sand, soil, and gravel dug up and removed from a shallow sea to deepen a sea-lane.

drift net: a long, wide fishing net that works like a broad curtain to trap everything swimming toward it.

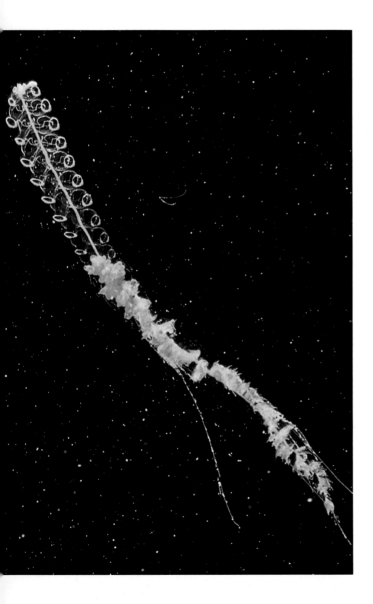

estuary (ESS-chuh-wair-ee): the place on a seacoast where a river's fresh water meets salt water from the sea.

evaporate: to change water from a liquid to a gas (vapor).

extinct: no longer existing.

fjord (fee-ORD): a long, narrow sea inlet bordered by steep cliffs.

food web: a series of plants and animals, each of which is a source of food for the next member in the web.

glacier (GLAY-sher): a huge mass of ice that moves slowly over land.

greenhouse effect: the result of the sun's heat becoming trapped in the earth's atmosphere by gases in the same way that glass traps heat in a greenhouse.

habitat: a natural setting that provides the necessities of life for plants and animals.

This siphonophore, a type of zooplankton, nourishes many other sea creatures in the food web.

high tide: the change in the ocean's level that occurs when the sea experiences a strong lunar (moon) pull. High tides bring ocean water to its highest level on the shore.

horizon: the line where the earth or ocean appears to meet the sky.

infiltration: the process by which water moves into and through underground soil and rocks.

krill: small, shrimplike animals that are the main food for toothless whales.

lagoon: a shallow body of water leading to or near the sea.

low tide: the change in the ocean's level that occurs when the sea experiences a weak lunar (moon) pull. At low tide, ocean water remains far from the shore.

nuclear waste: the dangerous radioactive materials from power stations that make nuclear energy and from factories that build nuclear weapons.

nutrient (NOO-tree-int): a substance used as food by plants or animals.

offshore well: an oil well or natural gas well that is anchored into the ocean floor.

overfishing: heavy and prolonged fishing that endangers future fish supplies.

Tugboats tow a Norwegian oil well to its offshore drilling site, where it will be anchored into the ocean floor.

ozone: a gas in the upper atmosphere that shields the earth from the sun's harmful rays.

phytoplankton (fight-o-PLANK-tin): plants of the plankton group that are moved in water by waves or currents.

plankton: plants and animals in water that are at the bottom of the food web.

poly-chlorinated biphenyls (PCBs): a group of toxic compounds used in the manufacture of plastics.

polyp (PAHL-ip): a marine animal shaped like a hollow tube that attaches one of its ends to a coral reef and uses the other end as its mouth.

purse seine (SAYN): a large, curved net designed to be set around a very large group of fish. When the upper ends of the net are brought together, the bottom of the net closes.

raw sewage: untreated household or industrial waste water and solids.

sea anemone (eh-NEM-eh-nee): a reef-dwelling creature whose fingerlike tentacles make it look like a flower.

sewage sludge: the solid materials left over after water from households and industries has been cleaned.

sound: a long, broad passage of water.

species (SPEE-sheez): a kind of living thing.

strait: a narrow stretch of sea that links two larger seas.

tide: the alternate rising and falling of the surface of the ocean caused by the position of the moon and sun in relation to the earth.

toxic algae: tiny, rootless water plants that contain poisons. When eaten by other life forms, the plants can be harmful or deadly.

transpiration: the movement of water through a plant's roots and leaves and out again into the air.

tropics: the hot, wet region that forms a broad belt around the equator.

tsunami (soo-NAHM-ee): a huge ocean wave that is caused by an underwater earthquake or volcano.

water cycle: the various paths and forms that water takes as it circulates through the air to the earth and back again.

zooplankton (zoh-uh-PLANK-tin): animals of the plankton group that can move themselves in water.

INDEX